fresh
fish
&seafood

D1613042

MARKS &
SPENCER

fresh

fish
& seafood

Marks and Spencer p.l.c.
PO Box 3339
Chester, CH99 9QS

www.marksandspencer.com

ISBN: 1-84461-286-4

Printed in Singapore

This edition designed by Shelley Doyle

Photography and text by The Bridgewater Book Company Ltd

Cover Photography by Mark Wood

Cover Home Economist Pamela Gwyther

NOTES FOR THE READER

This book uses both metric and imperial measurements. Follow the same units of measurement throughout; do not mix metric and imperial.

All spoon measurements are level: teaspoons are assumed to be 5 ml, and tablespoons are assumed to be 15 ml.

Unless otherwise stated, milk is assumed to be full fat and eggs are medium.

Recipes using raw or very lightly cooked eggs should be avoided by infants, the elderly, pregnant women, convalescents and anyone suffering from an illness.

Optional ingredients, variations or serving suggestions have not been included in the calculations. The times given are an approximate guide only. Preparation times differ according to the techniques used by different people and the cooking times may also vary from those given.

contents

Introduction

Anyone who has visited a seaside town and enjoyed lunch at a local restaurant serving the best of the morning's catch will know the uniquely delicious flavour of fish fresh from the sea. Indeed, it is hardly surprising that many of the best-loved fish and seafood dishes from around the world have their origins in just this situation. On America's East coast, New England and Manhattan created a wonderful soupy stew with local fish and native clams, producing what is now known as chowder. In the Mediterranean, the same process resulted in a very different, but equally fabulous dish known variously as bouillabaisse in France, brodetta in Italy and kakavia in Greece.

There are several good reasons for using fish and seafood when they are as fresh as possible. The flavour is incomparable and, equally important, the texture is superb. Even with refrigeration the flesh begins to deteriorate rapidly. Before it 'goes off' and is therefore actually harmful, it becomes much less pleasant. Many will have experienced the acute disappointment of eating a perfectly healthy prawn that closely resembles cotton wool. Fortunately, in these days of fast transportation and sustainable fish farming, stocks reach the shops astonishingly rapidly. Nevertheless, it is always best to buy fish and seafood on the day that you plan to eat it.

Because of its delicate flavour, fish is almost always at its best when it's at its simplest. Elaborate sauces, which disguise its natural flavour, are mostly out of fashion. This accords well with guidelines for healthy eating – doubly so, as fish itself is nutritionally excellent.

Soups & Stews

Warm and comforting, soups and stews reveal the versatility of fish and seafood. Fresh ingredients are crucial, despite the simmering needed for many recipes. Perfect flavours depend upon the best possible ingredients. Try Fish & Seafood Chowder for a true taste experience.

350 g/12 oz crab meat

4 tbsp butter

225 ml/8 fl oz milk

1 large shallot, very finely chopped

4 tbsp plain flour

300 ml/10 fl oz fish stock

300 ml/10 fl oz whipping or double cream

4 tbsp dry Oloroso sherry, or to taste

finely chopped fresh parsley, to garnish

crab soup

easy — serves 4

Pick over the crab meat to remove any bits of shell. Melt 1 tablespoon of the butter in a small saucepan over a very low heat. Add the crab meat, stir gently and add half the milk. Heat until bubbles appear around the edge and steam rises. Remove from the heat and set aside.

Melt the remaining butter in a large saucepan over a low heat. Add the shallot and cook gently for about 10 minutes until softened, stirring frequently; do not allow it to brown.

Stir in the flour and cook for 2 minutes. Whisk in the stock and remaining milk and bring to the boil, stirring constantly.

Gradually stir in the cream and season with salt and pepper to taste. Reduce the heat and simmer gently, stirring occasionally, for 10–15 minutes, until the shallots are soft and the soup is smooth and thick.

Stir in the crab meat mixture. If a thinner soup is preferred, add a little more stock or milk. Stir in the sherry and simmer for about 5 minutes until heated through. Taste and adjust the seasoning, if necessary. Ladle the soup into warm bowls and garnish with parsley.

1 litre/1^3/$_4$ pints fish stock
juice of ^{1}/$_2$ lime
2 tbsp rice wine or sherry
1 leek, trimmed and sliced
2 shallots, finely chopped
1 tbsp grated fresh root ginger
1 red chilli, deseeded and finely chopped
225 g/8 oz prawns, peeled and deveined
225 g/8 oz scallops
1^1/$_2$ tbsp chopped fresh flat-leafed parsley
salt and pepper

fresh flat-leaved parsley, chopped,
  to garnish

very easy - serves 4

Put the stock, lime juice, rice wine or sherry, leek, shallots, ginger and chilli into a large saucepan. Bring to the boil, then lower the heat, cover and simmer for 10 minutes.

Add the prawns, scallops and parsley, season with salt and pepper, and cook for about 1–2 minutes.

Remove the pan from the heat, ladle the soup into serving bowls, garnish with chopped fresh parsley and serve.

thai prawn & scallop soup

salmon bisque

1–2 salmon heads (depending on size) or a tail piece of salmon weighing about 500 g/1 lb 2 oz

900 ml/1 1/2 pints

1 fresh or dried bay leaf

1 lemon, sliced

a few black peppercorns

30 g/1 oz butter or margarine

2 tbsp finely chopped onion or spring onions

30 g/1 oz plain flour

150 ml/1/4 pint dry white wine or fish stock

150 ml/1/4 pint single cream

1 tbsp chopped fresh fennel or dill

2–3 tsp lemon or lime juice

salt and pepper

30–45 g/1–1 1/2 oz smoked salmon pieces, chopped (optional) and sprigs of fresh fennel or dill, to garnish

very easy - serves 4

Put the salmon, water, bay leaf, lemon and peppercorns into a saucepan. Bring to the boil, remove any scum from the surface, then cover the pan and simmer gently for 20 minutes until the fish is cooked through.

Remove from the heat, strain the stock and reserve 600 ml/1 pint. Remove and discard all the skin and bones from the salmon and flake the flesh, removing all the pieces from the head, if using.

Melt the butter or margarine in a saucepan and fry the onion or spring onions gently for about 5 minutes until soft. Stir in the flour and cook for 1 minute then stir in the reserved stock and wine or fish stock. Bring to the boil, stirring. Add the salmon, season well, then simmer gently for about 5 minutes.

Add the cream and the chopped fennel or dill and reheat gently, but do not boil. Sharpen to taste with lemon or lime juice and season again. Serve hot or chilled, garnished with smoked salmon (if using) and sprigs of fennel or dill.

smoked haddock soup

225 g/8 oz smoked haddock fillet

1 onion, chopped finely

1 garlic clove, crushed

600 ml/1 pint water

600 ml/1 pint skimmed milk

225–350 g/8–12 oz hot mashed potatoes

30 g/1 oz butter

about 1 tbsp lemon juice

6 tbsp low-fat natural fromage frais

4 tbsp fresh parsley, chopped

salt and pepper

easy – serves 4

Put the fish, onion, garlic and water into a saucepan. Bring to the boil, cover and simmer for 15–20 minutes.

Remove the fish from the pan, strip off the skin and remove all the bones. Flake the flesh finely.

Return the skin and bones to the cooking liquor and simmer for 10 minutes. Strain, discarding the skin and bone. Pour the liquor into a clean pan.

Add the milk, flaked fish and seasoning to the pan, bring to the boil and simmer for about 3 minutes.

Gradually whisk in sufficient mashed potato to give a fairly thick soup, then stir in the butter and sharpen to taste with lemon juice.

Add the fromage frais and 3 tablespoons of the chopped parsley. Reheat gently and adjust the seasoning. Sprinkle with the remaining parsley and serve immediately.

garlic fish soup

2 tsp olive oil

1 large onion, chopped

1 small fennel bulb, chopped

1 leek, sliced

3–4 large garlic cloves, thinly sliced

125 ml/4 fl oz dry white wine

1.2 litres/2 pints fish stock

4 tbsp white rice

1 strip pared lemon rind

1 bay leaf

450 g/1 lb skinless white fish fillets, cut into 4 cm/1^1/$_2$ inch pieces

50 ml/2 fl oz double cream

salt and pepper

2 tbsp chopped fresh parsley, to garnish

easy – serves 4

Heat the oil in a large saucepan over a medium-low heat. Add the onion, fennel, leek and garlic and cook for 4–5 minutes, stirring frequently, until the onion is softened.

Add the wine and bubble briefly. Add the stock, rice, lemon rind and bay leaf. Bring to the boil, reduce the heat to medium-low and simmer for 20–25 minutes, or until the rice and vegetables are soft. Remove the lemon rind and bay leaf.

Allow the soup to cool slightly, then transfer to a blender or food processor and purée until smooth, working in batches if necessary. (If using a food processor, strain off the cooking liquid and reserve. Purée the soup solids with enough cooking liquid to moisten them, then combine with the remaining liquid.)

Return the soup to the saucepan and bring to a simmer. Add the fish to the soup, cover and continue simmering gently, stirring occasionally, for 4–5 minutes, or until the fish is cooked and begins to flake.

Stir in the cream. Taste and adjust the seasoning, adding salt, if needed, and pepper. Ladle into warm bowls and serve sprinkled with parsley.

4 tbsp lemon juice

1 red chilli, deseeded and finely sliced

pinch of nutmeg

250 g/9 oz cod fillets, skinned

1 tbsp vegetable oil

1 onion, chopped

4 spring onions, trimmed and chopped

2 garlic cloves, chopped

450 g/1 lb sweet potatoes, diced

1 litre/$1^3/_4$ pints vegetable stock

salt and pepper

1 carrot, sliced

150 g/$5^1/_2$ oz white cabbage, shredded

2 celery sticks, trimmed and sliced

fresh crusty bread, to serve

very easy — serves 4

Put the lemon juice, chilli and nutmeg into a shallow, non-metallic (glass or ceramic) dish and mix to make a marinade. Rinse the cod, cut it into chunks and add to the bowl. Turn in the marinade until coated. Cover with clingfilm and leave to marinate for 30 minutes.

Heat the oil in a large pan over a medium heat. Add the onion and spring onions and cook, stirring, for 4 minutes. Add the garlic and cook for 2 minutes.

Add the sweet potato, pour in the stock and season. Bring to the boil, lower the heat, cover and simmer for 10 minutes. Add the carrot, cabbage and celery, season again, and simmer for 8–10 minutes. Remove from the heat and allow to cool a little.

Process the soup in a food processor until smooth (you may need to do this in batches), then return to the pan. Add the fish chunks and marinade and bring gently to the boil. Lower the heat and simmer for 10 minutes. Ladle the soup into bowls and serve with crusty bread.

cod & sweet potato soup

mediterranean fish soup

1 tbsp olive oil

1 large onion, chopped

2 garlic cloves, finely chopped

425 ml/15 fl oz fresh fish stock

150 ml/5 fl oz dry white wine

1 bay leaf

1 sprig each fresh thyme, rosemary and oregano

450 g/1 lb firm white fish fillets (such as cod, monkfish or halibut), skinned and cut into 2.5 cm/1 inch cubes

450 g/1 lb fresh mussels, prepared

400 g/14 oz can chopped tomatoes

225 g/8 oz peeled prawns, thawed if frozen

salt and pepper

sprigs of thyme, to garnish

lemon wedges and 4 slices toasted French bread, rubbed with cut garlic clove, to serve

easy – serves 4

Heat the olive oil in a large saucepan and gently fry the onion and garlic for 2–3 minutes until just softened.

Pour in the stock and wine and bring to the boil.

Tie the bay leaf and herbs together with clean string and add to the saucepan together with the fish and mussels. Stir well, cover and simmer for 5 minutes.

Stir in the tomatoes and prawns and continue to cook for a further 3–4 minutes until piping hot and the fish is cooked through.

Discard the herbs and any mussels that have not opened. Season to taste, then ladle into warm bowls.

Garnish with sprigs of fresh thyme and serve with lemon wedges and toasted bread.

fish soup with wontons

125 g/4¹/₂ oz large, cooked, peeled prawns

1 tsp chopped chives

1 small garlic clove, finely chopped

1 tbsp vegetable oil

12 wonton wrappers

1 small egg, beaten

850 ml/1¹/₂ pints fish stock

175 g/6 oz white fish fillet, diced

dash of chilli sauce

sliced fresh red chilli and chives,
   to garnish

easy — serves 4

Roughly chop a quarter of the prawns and mix together with the chopped chives and garlic.

Heat the oil in a preheated wok or large frying pan until it is really hot.

Stir-fry the prawn mixture for 1–2 minutes. Remove from the heat and set aside to cool completely.

Spread out the wonton wrappers on a work surface. Spoon a little of the prawn filling into the centre of each wrapper. Brush the edges of the wrappers with beaten egg and press the edges together, scrunching

them to form a 'moneybag' shape. Set aside while you are preparing the soup.

Pour the fish stock into a large saucepan and bring to the boil. Add the diced white fish and the remaining prawns and cook for 5 minutes.

Season to taste with the chilli sauce. Add the wontons and cook for a further 5 minutes.

Spoon into warmed serving bowls, garnish with sliced red chilli and chives and serve immediately.

fish & seafood chowder

1 kg/2 lb 4 oz live mussels
1 large onion, thinly sliced
2 garlic cloves, chopped
3 bay leaves
few sprigs of fresh parsley
few sprigs of fresh thyme
300 ml/10 fl oz water
225 g/8 oz smoked haddock fillets
500 g/1 lb 2 oz potatoes, peeled and diced
4 celery sticks, thickly sliced
600 ml/1 pint water
250 g/9 oz canned sweetcorn kernels, drained
  and rinsed
150 ml/5 fl oz low-fat natural yogurt
1 tsp cornflour
150 ml/5 fl oz dry white wine, or dry cider
$^1/_2$ tsp cayenne pepper, or to taste
salt and pepper
2 tbsp chopped fresh parsley

warm crusty bread, to serve

easy - serves 4

Scrub the mussels, pull off any beards that are attached to them, then rinse thoroughly. Discard any mussels that do not close when sharply tapped with the back of a knife.

Place the onion, garlic, herbs, water and mussels in a large saucepan. Cover and cook over a high heat, shaking the saucepan occasionally, for 5 minutes, or until the mussels have opened.

Line a colander with muslin or cheesecloth and sieve the mussel and liquid into a bowl. When the mussels are cool enough to handle, remove from their shells. Discard any mussels that are closed. Reserve the liquid.

Place the haddock and vegetables in a large saucepan, add the water, cover and simmer for 10 minutes. Remove the fish, then skin, bone and flake it. Sieve the cooking liquid into the seafood liquid and reserve the vegetables. Return the cooking liquid to the rinsed-out saucepan, add the sweetcorn and bring to the boil.

Stir the yogurt and cornflour together, then stir in a little of the fish liquid. Pour it into the saucepan and stir well then add the reserved fish and vegetables. Add the wine, season with cayenne and pepper and heat the soup gently. Season to taste and transfer to a serving plate. Sprinkle with the parsley and serve with crusty bread.

3 tbsp olive oil
2 garlic cloves, chopped
3 spring onions, trimmed and chopped
1 red pepper, deseeded and chopped
425 g/15 oz canned chopped tomatoes
1 tbsp tomato purée
1 bay leaf
$1/2$ tsp dried mixed herbs
200 g/7 oz live mussels
150 g/$5^{1}/2$ oz cod fillet, skinned
150 g/$5^{1}/2$ oz swordfish steak, skinned
350 ml/12 fl oz fish stock
4 tbsp red wine
salt and pepper
200 g/7 oz canned crab meat
200 g/7 oz prawns, peeled and deveined
250 g/9 oz cooked lobster meat

fresh flat-leafed parsley chopped, and slices of
  lemon, to garnish

slices of French bread, to serve

easy - serves 4

Heat the oil in a pan over a low heat. Add the garlic, spring onions and red pepper and cook, stirring, for 4 minutes. Add the tomatoes, tomato purée, bay leaf and mixed herbs. Cook for 10 minutes.

Meanwhile, soak the mussels in lightly salted water for 10 minutes. Scrub under cold running water and pull off any beards. Discard any with broken shells. Tap the remaining mussels and discard any that refuse to close. Put them in a large pan with a little water, bring to the boil and cook over a high heat for 4 minutes. Remove from the heat, drain and discard any mussels that remain closed.

Cut the cod and swordfish into chunks and add to the tomato pan. Add the stock and wine. Season and bring to the boil. Add the mussels and crab, lower the heat, cover and cook for 5 minutes. Add the prawns and cook for 3 minutes. Cut the lobster into chunks, add to the pan and cook for 2 minutes. Transfer to bowls, garnish with parsley and lemon slices and serve with slices of French bread.

fruits de mer stew

Light & Healthy

The health benefits of fish are now widely celebrated and simplicity is very much in vogue when it comes to fish suppers. Buy the freshest fish possible and you will be rewarded with the most flavoursome and delicate dishes imaginable. Try Grilled Sardines with Lemon and Coriander for guilt-free pleasure.

monkfish & asparagus stir-fry

500 g/1 lb 2 oz monkfish

4 tbsp vegetable oil

2 courgettes, trimmed, halved and sliced

1 red pepper, deseeded and sliced

2 garlic cloves, finely chopped

150 g/5$\frac{1}{2}$ oz fresh asparagus spears

100 g/3$\frac{1}{2}$ oz mangetouts

6 tbsp plain flour

4 tbsp lemon sauce (available ready-made from supermarkets and oriental food shops)

1 tbsp freshly grated lemon-grass

1 tbsp grated fresh root ginger

salt and pepper

very easy – serves 4

Remove any membrane from the monkfish, then cut the flesh into thin slices. Cover with clingfilm and set aside. Heat 2 tablespoons of the oil in a wok or large frying pan until hot. Add the courgettes and stir-fry for 2 minutes. Add the red pepper and garlic and cook for another 2 minutes. Add the asparagus and cook for 1 minute, then add the mangetouts and cook for 2 minutes. Transfer the vegetables onto a plate.

Put the flour in a shallow dish and turn the fish slices in the flour until coated. Heat the remaining oil in the wok or frying pan. Add the fish and stir-fry for 5 minutes, or until cooked to your taste (you may need to do this in batches). Transfer the fish to another plate.

Put the lemon sauce, lemon-grass and ginger in the wok or frying pan. Add the fish and stir-fry over a medium heat for a few seconds. Add the vegetables and stir-fry for 1 minute. Season, stir again and remove from the heat. Transfer to warm plates and serve.

250 g/9 oz canned or freshly cooked crab meat

1 red pepper, deseeded and chopped

4 tomatoes, chopped

3 spring onions, trimmed and chopped

1 tbsp chopped fresh flat-leafed parsley

1 red chilli, deseeded and chopped

3 tbsp lime juice

3 tbsp orange juice

salt and pepper

sprigs of fresh flat-leafed parsley, and wedges of lime, to garnish

carrots and celery, cut into matchsticks, and tortilla chips, to serve

very easy — serves 4

Put the crab meat, red pepper, tomatoes, spring onions, parsley and chilli into a large non-metallic (glass or ceramic) bowl, which will not react with acid. Add the lime juice and orange juice, season with salt and pepper and mix well. Cover with clingfilm and refrigerate for 30 minutes to allow the flavours to combine.

Remove the salsa from the refrigerator. Garnish with parsley sprigs and wedges of lime and serve with carrots, celery and tortilla chips for dipping.

crab & citrus salsa

giant garlic **prawns**

125 ml/4 fl oz olive oil

4 garlic cloves, finely chopped

2 hot fresh red chillies, deseeded and finely chopped

450 g/1 lb cooked king prawns

2 tbsp chopped fresh flat-leaf parsley

salt and pepper

lemon wedges, to garnish

extremely easy – serves 4

Heat the oil in a large heavy-based frying pan over a low heat. Add the garlic and chillies and cook, stirring occasionally, for 1–2 minutes, or until softened, but not coloured.

Add the prawns and stir-fry for 2–3 minutes, or until heated through and coated in the oil and garlic mixture.

Turn off the heat and add the chopped parsley, stirring well to mix. Season to taste with salt and pepper.

Divide the prawns and garlic-flavoured oil between warmed serving dishes and garnish with lemon wedges and serve.

scallops on skewers

48 prepared scallops, thawed if frozen

juice of 1 lemon

24 slices of prosciutto

olive oil, for brushing

mixed salad leaves

pepper

lemon wedges, to garnish

extremely easy - serves 4

Preheat the grill to medium. Sprinkle the scallops with the lemon juice. Cut the prosciutto into strips, then wrap a strip around each scallop and thread them onto presoaked wooden skewers, 3–4 at a time.

Brush the scallops with olive oil and place them on a large baking sheet. Cook under the preheated grill for 4 minutes on each side, or until the scallops are opaque and tender.

Make a bed of mixed salad leaves on individual serving plates and divide the skewers between them. Season to taste with pepper, garnish with lemon wedges and serve.

tuna & herbed fusilli salad

200 g/7 oz dried fusilli

1 red pepper, deseeded and cut into quarters

150 g/5$\frac{1}{2}$ oz fresh asparagus spears

1 red onion, sliced

4 tomatoes, sliced

200 g/7 oz canned tuna in brine, drained

DRESSING

6 tbsp basil-flavoured oil or extra-virgin olive oil

3 tbsp white wine vinegar

1 tbsp lime juice

1 tsp mustard

1 tsp honey

4 tbsp chopped fresh basil

sprigs of fresh basil, to garnish

extremely easy – serves 4

Bring a large pan of lightly salted water to the boil. Cook the fusilli for 10 minutes, or according to the instructions on the packet. The pasta should be tender but still firm to the bite. While it is cooking, put the pepper quarters under a grill and cook until the skins have begun to blacken. Transfer to a polythene bag, seal and set aside.

Bring another pan of water to the boil and cook the asparagus for 4 minutes. Drain and plunge into cold water, then drain again. Remove the pasta from the heat, drain and set aside to cool. Take the red pepper quarters from the bag and remove the blackened skins. Slice the peppers into strips.

To make the dressing, put all the ingredients into a large bowl and stir together well. Add the pasta, pepper strips, asparagus, onion, tomatoes and tuna. Toss together gently then divide between serving bowls. Garnish with sprigs of fresh basil and serve.

12 sardines, scaled and gutted

1 tbsp olive oil

DRESSING

1 garlic clove, finely chopped

3 spring onions, trimmed and sliced

125 ml/4 fl oz extra-virgin olive oil

4 tbsp lemon juice

2 tbsp white wine vinegar

4 tbsp chopped fresh coriander

pepper

slices of fresh lemon and sprigs of fresh coriander, to serve

very easy – serves 4

Preheat the grill to medium. Rinse the fish inside and out under cold running water. Drain, then pat dry with kitchen paper.

To make the dressing, put the garlic, spring onions, olive oil, lemon juice, vinegar and coriander into a small bowl and mix together well. Season with plenty of pepper and set aside.

Line a grill pan with aluminium foil, then brush the foil with a little olive oil. Arrange the sardines on the foil, then spoon some of the dressing inside each fish. Brush more dressing on the top of the sardines and cook under the preheated grill for about 3 minutes. Turn the fish over, brush with more dressing and cook for a further 3 minutes, or until cooked through.

Remove from the grill, transfer onto individual serving plates and garnish with lemon slices and coriander sprigs.

grilled sardines with lemon & coriander

pasta **niçoise** salad

225 g/8 oz farfalle

175 g/6 oz French beans, topped and tailed

350 g/12 oz fresh tuna steaks

115 g/4 oz baby plum tomatoes, halved

8 anchovy fillets, drained on absorbent kitchen paper

2 tbsp capers in brine, drained

25 g/1 oz pitted black olives in brine, drained

salt and pepper

DRESSING

1 tbsp olive oil

1 garlic clove, crushed

1 tbsp lemon juice

$\frac{1}{2}$ tsp finely grated lemon rind

1 tbsp shredded

fresh basil leaves, to garnish

easy - serves 4

Cook the pasta in lightly salted boiling water according to the instructions on the packet until just cooked. Drain well, set aside and keep warm.

Bring a small saucepan of lightly salted water to the boil and cook the French beans for 5–6 minutes until just tender. Drain well and toss into the pasta. Set aside and keep warm.

Preheat the grill to medium. Rinse and pat the tuna steaks dry on absorbent kitchen paper. Season on both sides with black pepper. Place the tuna steaks on the grill rack and cook for 4–5 minutes on each side until cooked through.

Drain the tuna on absorbent kitchen paper and flake into bite-sized pieces. Toss the tuna into the pasta along with the tomatoes, anchovies, capers and olives. Set aside and keep warm.

Meanwhile, prepare the dressing. Mix all the ingredients together and season well. Pour the dressing over the pasta mixture and mix carefully. Transfer to a warmed serving bowl and serve sprinkled with fresh basil leaves.

thai potato **crab cakes**

450 g/1 lb floury potatoes, diced

175 g/6 oz white crab meat, drained if canned

4 spring onions, chopped

1 tsp light soy sauce

1/2 tsp sesame oil

1 tsp chopped lemon-grass

1 tsp lime juice

3 tbsp plain flour

2 tbsp vegetable oil

salt and pepper

SAUCE

4 tbsp finely chopped cucumber

2 tbsp clear honey

1 tbsp garlic wine vinegar

1/2 tsp light soy sauce

1 chopped red chilli

1 red chilli, sliced, and cucumber slices, to garnish

very easy - serves 4

Preheat the barbecue. Rinse the fish steaks under cold running water and pat dry with kitchen paper.

Mix the paprika, thyme, cayenne, black and white pepper, salt and allspice together in a shallow dish.

Place the butter and sunflower oil in a small saucepan and heat gently, stirring occasionally, until the butter melts.

Brush the butter mixture liberally all over the fish steaks, on both sides, then dip the fish into the spicy mix until coated on both sides.

Cook the fish over hot coals for 3 minutes, on each side until cooked through. Continue to baste the fish with the remaining butter mixture during the cooking time.

smoked salmon, asparagus & avocado salad

200 g/7 oz fresh asparagus spears
1 large ripe avocado
1 tbsp lemon juice
large handful fresh rocket leaves
225 g/8 oz smoked salmon slices
1 red onion, finely sliced
1 tbsp chopped fresh parsley
1 tbsp chopped fresh chives

DRESSING
1 garlic clove, chopped
4 tbsp extra-virgin olive oil
2 tbsp white wine vinegar
1 tbsp lemon juice
pinch of sugar
1 tsp mustard

sprigs of fresh flat-leafed parsley and wedges of
 lemon, to garnish

fresh wholemeal bread, to serve

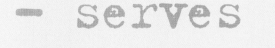

very easy – serves 4

Bring a large saucepan of salted water to the boil. Add the asparagus and cook for 4 minutes, then drain. Refresh under cold running water and drain again. Set aside to cool.

To make the dressing, combine all the ingredients in a small bowl and stir together well. Cut the avocado in half lengthways, then remove and discard the stone and skin. Cut the flesh into bite-sized pieces and brush with lemon juice to prevent discoloration.

To assemble the salad, arrange the rocket leaves on individual serving plates and top with the asparagus and avocado. Cut the smoked salmon into strips and scatter over the top of the salad, then scatter over the onion and herbs. Drizzle over the dressing, then garnish with fresh parsley sprigs and lemon wedges. Serve with fresh wholemeal bread.

1 tbsp chilli oil

1 large onion, roughly chopped

2 garlic cloves, chopped

250 g/9 oz canned or freshly cooked crab meat

1 small red chilli, deseeded and finely chopped

2 tomatoes, chopped

1 tbsp chopped fresh coriander

salt and pepper

8 small wheat or corn tortillas

sprigs of fresh coriander, to garnish

125 ml/4 fl oz soured cream, to serve

very easy – serves 4

Heat the oil in a frying pan and add the onion and garlic. Cook over a medium heat for about 3–4 minutes until the onion is slightly softened.

Add the crab meat, chilli, tomatoes and coriander. Season with salt and pepper. Cook, stirring, for 10 minutes, or according to your taste. About a minute before the crab is ready, warm the tortillas in a dry frying pan for a few seconds.

Remove the crab mixture and the tortillas from the heat. Spread a spoonful of soured cream onto each tortilla, add some of the crab mixture and roll up. Garnish with coriander sprigs and serve at once.

spicy **crab** tortillas

Family Favourites

Feeding the family with good food couldn't be simpler with this selection of contemporary and classic fish dishes. The fresh tastes you can create with simple recipes will keep everyone happy. Smoked Haddock Casserole combines subtle flavours with satisfying tastes.

fish
kedgeree

3 tbsp butter

2 shallots, chopped

1 leek, trimmed and finely sliced

300 g/10$\frac{1}{2}$ oz brown rice

600 ml/1 pint fish stock

200 g/7 oz salmon fillets

200 g/7 oz smoked haddock fillets

300 ml/10 fl oz milk

$\frac{1}{2}$ tsp garam masala

salt and pepper

finely shredded Chinese lettuce leaves, to garnish

fresh bread rolls, to serve

very easy – serves 4

Preheat the oven to 190°C/375°F/Gas Mark 5. Melt the butter in a large frying pan over a low heat. Add the shallots and leek and cook, stirring, for about 4 minutes until slightly softened. Add the rice, then stir in the stock and bring to the boil.

Transfer the shallot mixture to a large, ovenproof casserole dish. Cover and bake in the centre of the preheated oven for about 25 minutes, until all the liquid has been absorbed.

About 5 minutes before the end of the cooking time, rinse the fish fillets under cold running water, then pat dry with kitchen paper. Pour the milk into a saucepan and bring to the boil. Add the fish and poach for 5–6 minutes until tender.

Remove the rice from the oven. Drain the fish, discard the milk and flake the fillets into small pieces. Add the fish and garam masala to the rice, and season with salt and pepper. Stir together well and garnish with shredded Chinese lettuce leaves. Serve with bread rolls.

2 tbsp olive oil, plus extra for brushing

4 haddock fillets, about 175 g/6 oz each

grated rind and juice of 2 lemons

salt and pepper

115 g/4 oz Gruyère cheese, grated

4 tbsp fresh white breadcrumbs

4 tbsp crème fraîche

4 garlic cloves, finely chopped

lemon wedges and fresh parsley sprigs, to garnish

easy – serves 4

Preheat the oven to 200°C/400°F/Gas Mark 6. Brush a roasting tin or large ovenproof dish with olive oil and arrange the fish in it in a single layer. Sprinkle with a little lemon juice and season to taste with salt and pepper.

Mix the olive oil, cheese, breadcrumbs, crème fraîche, garlic, lemon rind and 6 tablespoons of the remaining lemon juice together in a large bowl and season to taste with salt and pepper. Spread the cheese paste evenly over the fish fillets.

Bake in the oven for 12–15 minutes, or until the fish is cooked through. Transfer to warmed serving plates, garnish with lemon wedges and parsley sprigs and serve immediately.

haddock in a cheese jacket

poached salmon

1 small onion, sliced

1 small carrot, sliced

1 stick celery, sliced

1 bay leaf

pared rind and juice of $^1/_2$ orange

a few stalks of parsley

salt

5-6 black peppercorns

700 ml/1$^1/_4$ pints water

4 salmon steaks, about 350 g/12 oz each

salad leaves, to serve

lemon twists, to garnish

SAUCE

1 large avocado, peeled, halved and stoned

125 ml/4 fl oz low-fat natural yogurt

grated zest and juice of $^1/_2$ orange

black pepper

a few drops of hot red pepper sauce

easy - serves 4

Put the onion, carrot, celery, bay leaf, orange rind, orange juice, parsley stalks, salt and peppercorns in a pan just large enough to take the salmon steaks in a single layer. Pour on the water, cover the pan and bring to the boil. Simmer the stock for 20 minutes.

Arrange the salmon steaks in the pan, return the stock to the boil and simmer for 3 minutes. Cover the pan, remove from the heat and leave the salmon to cool in the stock.

Roughly chop the avocado and place it in a blender or food processor with the yogurt, orange zest and orange juice. Process until smooth, then season to taste with salt, pepper and hot pepper sauce.

Remove the salmon steaks from the stock (reserve it to make fish soup or a sauce), skin them and pat dry with kitchen paper.

Cover the serving dish with salad leaves, arrange the salmon steaks on top and spoon a little of the sauce into the centre of each one. Garnish the fish with lemon twists, and serve the remaining sauce separately.

smoked haddock casserole

25 g/1 oz butter, plus extra for greasing

450 g/1 lb smoked haddock fillets, cut into 4 slices

600 ml/1 pint milk

25 g/1 oz plain flour

pinch of freshly grated nutmeg

3 tbsp double cream

1 tbsp chopped fresh parsley

2 eggs, hard boiled and mashed to a pulp

450 g/1 lb dried fusilli

1 tbsp lemon juice

salt and pepper

boiled new potatoes and beetroot, to serve

easy – serves 4

Thoroughly grease a casserole dish with butter. Put the haddock in the casserole dish and pour over the milk. Bake in a preheated oven at 200°C/400°F/Gas Mark 6 for about 15 minutes. Carefully pour the cooking liquid into a jug without breaking up the fish.

Melt the butter in a saucepan and stir in the flour. Gradually whisk in the reserved cooking liquid. Season to taste with salt, pepper and nutmeg. Stir in the cream, parsley and mashed egg and cook, stirring constantly, for 2 minutes.

Meanwhile, bring a large saucepan of lightly salted water to the boil. Add the fusilli and lemon juice and cook for 8–10 minutes until tender, but still firm to the bite.

Drain the pasta and spoon or tip it over the fish. Top with the egg sauce and return the casserole to the oven for 10 minutes.

Serve the casserole with boiled new potatoes and beetroot.

warm tuna & kidney bean salad

4 fresh tuna steaks, about 175 g/6 oz each

1 tbsp olive oil

salt and pepper

200 g/7 oz canned kidney beans

100 g/3$\frac{1}{2}$ oz canned sweetcorn

2 spring onions, trimmed and thinly sliced

DRESSING

5 tbsp extra-virgin olive oil

3 tbsp balsamic vinegar

1 tbsp lime juice

1 garlic clove, chopped

1 tbsp chopped fresh coriander

salt and pepper

sprigs of fresh coriander, and wedges of lime,
   to garnish

extremely easy – serves 4

Preheat a ridged griddle pan. While the pan is heating, brush the tuna steaks with olive oil, then season with salt and pepper. Cook the steaks for 2 minutes, then turn them over and cook on the other side for a further 2 minutes, or according to your taste, but do not overcook. Remove from the heat and allow to cool slightly.

While the tuna is cooling, heat the kidney beans and sweetcorn according to the instructions on the cans, then drain.

To make the dressing, put all the ingredients into a small bowl and stir together well.

Put the kidney beans, sweetcorn and spring onions into a large bowl, pour over half of the dressing and mix together well. Divide the bean and sweetcorn salad between individual serving plates, then place a tuna steak on each one. Drizzle over the remaining dressing, garnish with the fresh coriander sprigs and lime wedges, and serve.

350 g/12 oz haddock fillets, skinned and
  cut into small pieces
25 g/1 oz almonds, chopped
25 g/1 oz fresh breadcrumbs
½ onion, finely chopped
1 red chilli, deseeded and finely chopped
1 egg white
1 tbsp soy sauce
1 tbsp finely chopped lemon-grass
2 tbsp chopped fresh coriander
1 tbsp groundnut oil

hamburger buns, slices of tomato, and a selection of
  green salad leaves, to serve

very easy – serves 4

Put the haddock, almonds, breadcrumbs, onion, chilli, egg white, soy sauce, lemon-grass and coriander into a large bowl and stir together. Put the mixture into a food processor and process until thoroughly blended. Transfer to a clean work surface and, using your hands, shape the mixture into flat, round burger shapes.

Heat the oil in a frying pan and add the burgers. Cook for about 5 minutes, turning once, until cooked through.

Remove from the heat. Serve with hamburger buns stuffed with tomato slices and crisp lettuce, and a green side salad.

thai fish burgers

indian cod with tomatoes

3 tbsp vegetable oil

4 cod steaks, about 2.5 cm/1 inch thick

salt and pepper

1 onion, finely chopped

2 garlic cloves, crushed

1 red pepper, deseeded and chopped

1 tsp ground coriander

1 tsp ground cumin

1 tsp ground turmeric

½ tsp garam masala

400 g/14 oz canned chopped tomatoes

150 ml/5 fl oz coconut milk

1–2 tbsp chopped fresh coriander or parsley

very easy – serves 4

Heat the oil in a frying pan, add the fish steaks, season with salt and pepper and cook for 2–3 minutes, until browned on both sides but not cooked through. Remove from the pan and reserve.

Add the onion, garlic, red pepper and spices and cook over a very low heat for 2 minutes, stirring frequently. Add the tomatoes, bring to the boil and simmer for 5 minutes.

Add the fish steaks to the pan and simmer gently for 8 minutes, or until the fish is cooked through. Remove from the pan with a slotted spoon and keep warm on a serving dish.

Add the coconut milk and coriander to the pan and reheat gently. Spoon the sauce over the cod steaks and serve immediately.

prawn stir-fry

$^1/_2$ cucumber

2 tbsp sunflower oil

6 spring onions, halved lengthways and cut into 4 cm/1$^1/_2$ inch lengths

1 stalk lemon-grass, sliced thinly

1 garlic clove, chopped

1 tsp chopped fresh red chilli

125 g/4$^1/_2$ oz oyster mushrooms

1 tsp chopped ginger root

350 g/12 oz cooked peeled prawns

2 tsp cornflour

2 tbsp water

1 tbsp dark soy sauce

$^1/_2$ tsp fish sauce

2 tbsp dry sherry or rice wine

boiled rice, to serve

very easy - serves 4

Cut the cucumber into strips about 5 mm x 4 cm/ $^1/_4$ x 1$^3/_4$ inches.

Heat the sunflower oil in a wok or large frying pan.

Add the spring onions, cucumber, lemon-grass, garlic, chilli, oyster mushrooms and ginger to the wok or frying pan and stir-fry for 2 minutes.

Add the prawns and stir-fry for a further minute.

Mix together the cornflour, water, soy sauce and fish sauce until smooth.

Stir the cornflour mixture and sherry or wine into the wok and heat through, stirring, until the sauce has thickened. Serve with rice.

450 g/1 lb finnan haddock, filleted, skin removed and
  flesh flaked

115 g/ 4 oz prawns

115 g/4 oz sole fillet, skin removed and flesh sliced

juice of 1 lemon

60 g/2 oz butter

3 leeks, very thinly sliced

60 g/2 oz plain flour

about 600 ml/1 pint milk

2 tbsp clear honey

200g/7 oz grated Mozzarella cheese

450g/1 lb pre-cooked lasagne

60 g/2 oz freshly grated Parmesan cheese

pepper

seafood lasagne

easy - serves 4

Put the haddock fillet, prawns and sole fillet into a large bowl and season with pepper and lemon juice according to taste. Set aside while you make the sauce.

Melt the butter in a large saucepan. Add the leeks and cook, stirring occasionally, for 8 minutes. Add the flour and cook, stirring constantly, for 1 minute. Gradually stir in enough milk to make a thick, creamy sauce.

Blend in the honey and Mozzarella cheese and cook for a further 3 minutes. Remove the pan from the heat and mix in the fish and prawns.

Make alternate layers of fish sauce and lasagne in an ovenproof dish, finishing with a layer of fish sauce on top. Generously sprinkle over the grated Parmesan cheese and bake in a preheated oven at 180°C/350°F/Gas Mark 4 for 30 minutes. Serve immediately.

1 tsp black peppercorns

1 tsp fennel seeds

1 tsp cayenne pepper

1 tsp dried oregano

1 tsp dried thyme

3 garlic cloves, finely chopped

2 tbsp polenta

4 monkfish fillets, about 175 g/6 oz each, skinned

3 tbsp corn oil

thinly pared strips of lime rind, and lime halves,
    to garnish

very easy - serves 4

Crush the peppercorns lightly in a mortar with a pestle. Mix the peppercorns, fennel seeds, cayenne, oregano, thyme, garlic and polenta in a shallow dish.

Place the monkfish, 1 fillet at a time, in the spice mixture and press gently to coat all over. Shake off any excess.

Heat the corn oil in a large, heavy-based frying pan. Add the monkfish and cook for 3–4 minutes on each side, or until tender and cooked through. Serve garnished with the lime rind and lime halves.

blackened fish

Special Occasions

Special Occasions

Good fish dishes spell sophistication, and here simple recipes will bring the highest reward. Make an impression with chic cuisine that is as easy as it is effective. Buy the best fish and seafood possible for Lobster Thermidor or Red Mullet with Chermoula.

2 cooked lobsters, about 750 g/1 lb 10 oz each

55 g/2 oz butter

1 shallot, chopped

25 g/1 oz plain flour

300 ml/10 fl oz milk

1½ tsp chopped fresh chervil

1 tsp chopped fresh tarragon

1½ tsp chopped fresh parsley

2 tsp Dijon mustard

salt and pepper

6 tbsp dry white wine

3 tbsp double cream

4 tbsp freshly grated Parmesan cheese

lemon slices and fresh parsley sprigs, to garnish

lobster thermidor

easy – serves 4

Preheat the grill to medium. Twist off and discard the lobster heads and pull off the claws. Crack the claws with a small hammer and remove the flesh. Using a sharp knife, split the lobsters in half lengthways and remove and discard the intestinal vein. Remove the flesh and reserve. Scrub the half-shells under cold running water and drain upside down on kitchen paper. Cut the lobster flesh into 2-cm/³⁄4-inch thick slices.

Melt the butter in a heavy-based saucepan. Add the shallot and cook over a low heat for 4–5 minutes, or until softened. Sprinkle in the flour and cook, stirring constantly, for 2 minutes. Remove the saucepan from the heat and gradually stir in the milk. Return the saucepan to the heat and bring to the boil, stirring. Cook, stirring, until thickened and smooth.

Reduce the heat, stir in the herbs and mustard and season to taste with salt and pepper. Remove the saucepan from the heat and whisk in the wine and cream. Return to a low heat and simmer until thickened. Add the lobster flesh and heat through for 2–3 minutes.

Divide the mixture between the half-shells and sprinkle with the Parmesan cheese. Cook under the hot grill until the topping is golden and bubbling. Serve, garnished with lemon slices and parsley.

500 g/1 lb 2 oz sea bream or perch fillets

1 garlic clove, finely chopped

1 small red chilli, deseeded and finely chopped

2 tbsp Thai fish sauce (nam pla)

3 tbsp lemon juice

100 ml/3½ fl oz fish stock

3 spring onions, trimmed and finely sliced

1 tbsp finely grated lemon rind

1 tbsp finely grated fresh root ginger

sprigs of coriander and wedges of lemon, to garnish

freshly cooked egg noodles, and fresh bread rolls
  (optional), to serve

easy — serves 4

Rinse the fish fillets under cold running water, then pat dry with kitchen paper. Make several fairly deep diagonal cuts into the fish on both sides. Put the fish on a heatproof plate that is slightly smaller than your wok. The plate should have a rim.

In a separate bowl, mix together the garlic, chilli, fish sauce, lemon juice and stock. Pour this mixture over the fish. Scatter over the spring onions, lemon rind and ginger.

Fill a large wok with boiling water up to a depth of about 4 cm/1½ inches. Bring it back to the boil, then set a rack or trivet inside the wok. Put the plate of fish on top of the rack, then cover the wok with a lid. Lower the heat a little and steam the fish for about 10 minutes, or until cooked through.

Lift out the fish and arrange on the freshly cooked egg noodles. Garnish with coriander sprigs and lemon wedges, and serve with fresh bread rolls (if using).

steamed **sea bream** with ginger

red **mullet** with chermoula

4 garlic cloves

sea salt

55 g/2 oz chopped fresh coriander

2 tsp paprika

2 tsp ground cumin

pinch of chilli powder

150 ml/5 fl oz olive oil

4 tbsp lemon or lime juice

8 x 175 g/6 oz or 4 x 350 g/12 oz red mullet or snapper, cleaned and scaled

fresh coriander sprigs and lime wedges, to garnish

very easy - serves 4

Begin by preparing the chermoula. Pound the garlic with a pinch of sea salt in a mortar with a pestle. Gradually work in the coriander and spices. Transfer to a bowl and gradually whisk in the oil, then the lemon juice.

Make 3–4 diagonal slashes on both sides of the fish. Rub the chermoula into the slashes. Place the

fish in a non-metallic dish, cover and marinate in the refrigerator for 1 hour.

Preheat the grill or barbecue. Cook the fish for 4–5 minutes on each side, until the flesh flakes easily. Serve immediately, garnished with coriander sprigs and lime wedges.

noodles with chilli & **prawns**

250 g/9 oz thin glass noodles

2 tbsp sunflower oil

1 onion, sliced

2 red chillies, deseeded and very finely chopped

4 lime leaves, thinly shredded

1 tbsp fresh coriander

2 tbsp palm or caster sugar

2 tbsp fish sauce

450 g/1 lb raw tiger prawns, peeled

very easy — serves 4

Place the noodles in a large bowl. Pour over enough boiling water to cover the noodles and leave to stand for 5 minutes. Drain thoroughly and set aside until required.

Heat the sunflower oil in a large preheated wok or frying pan until it is really hot.

Add the onion, red chillies and lime leaves to the wok and stir-fry for 1 minute.

Add the coriander, palm or caster sugar, fish sauce and prawns to the wok or frying pan and stir-fry for a further 2 minutes or until the prawns turn pink.

Add the drained noodles to the wok, toss to mix well, and stir-fry for 1–2 minutes or until heated through.

Transfer the noodles and prawns to warm serving bowls and serve immediately.

smoked trout with pears

55 g/2 oz watercress

1 head of radicchio, torn into pieces

4 smoked trout fillets, skinned

2 ripe pears, such as Williams

2 tbsp lemon juice

2 tbsp extra-virgin olive oil

salt and pepper

3 tbsp soured cream

2 tsp creamed horseradish

thinly sliced buttered brown bread, crusts removed,
  to serve

extremely easy - serves 4

Place the watercress and radicchio in a bowl. Cut the trout fillets into thin strips and add to the bowl. Halve and core the pears, then slice thinly. Place in a separate bowl, add 4 teaspoons of the lemon juice and toss to coat. Add the pears to the salad.

To make the dressing, mix the remaining lemon juice and the olive oil together in a bowl, then season to taste with salt and pepper. Pour the dressing over the salad and toss well. Transfer to a large salad bowl.

Mix the soured cream and horseradish together in a separate bowl until thoroughly blended, then spoon over the salad. Serve with buttered brown bread.

2 small cooked crabs

2 tbsp vegetable oil

9-cm/3-inch piece fresh root ginger, grated

2 garlic cloves, thinly sliced

1 green pepper, seeded and cut into thin strips

6 spring onions, cut into 2.5-cm/1-inch lengths

2 tbsp dry sherry

$1/2$ tsp sesame oil

150 ml/$1/4$ pint fish stock

1 tsp light brown sugar

2 tsp cornflour

150 ml/$1/4$ pint water

easy – serves 4

Rinse the crabs and gently loosen around the shell at the top. Using a sharp knife, cut away the grey tissue and discard. Rinse the crabs again.

Twist off the legs and claws from the crabs. Using a pair of crab claw crackers or a cleaver, gently crack the claws to break through the shell to expose the flesh. Remove and discard any loose pieces of shell.

Separate the body and discard the inedible lungs and sac. Cut down the centre of each crab to separate the body into two pieces and then cut each of these in half again.

Heat the oil in a preheated wok. Add the ginger and garlic and stir-fry for 1 minute. Add the crab pieces and stir-fry for a further minute.

Stir in the pepper, spring onions, sherry, sesame oil, stock and sugar. Bring to the boil, reduce the heat, cover and simmer for 3–4 minutes.

Blend the cornflour with the water and stir into the wok. Bring to the boil, stirring, until the sauce is thickened and clear. Transfer to a warm serving dish and serve immediately.

crab in ginger sauce

halibut with caramelised onions

1 tbsp vegetable oil
½ small onion, sliced thinly
½ tsp balsamic vinegar
1 tbsp butter, melted
115 g/4 oz halibut fillet or steak

very easy – serves 1

Heat the oil over a medium heat in a large frying pan. Add the onions, stir well and reduce the heat. Cook for 15–20 minutes on a very low heat, stirring occasionally, until the onions are very soft and brown.

Add the vinegar to the onions and cook for 2 minutes longer, stirring constantly to prevent sticking.

Brush melted butter over the fish.

Preheat the grill or a griddle that goes on top of the cooker. Sear the fish on high, then reduce the heat and cook for about 10 minutes, turning once. Cooking time depends on the thickness of the fillet, but the fish should be firm and tender when done.

Remove the fish from the heat, place on a serving platter and top with the caramelised onions.

salmon yakitori

350 g/12 oz chunky salmon fillet

8 baby leeks

YAKITORI SAUCE

5 tbsp light soy sauce

5 tbsp fish stock

2 tbsp caster sugar

5 tbsp dry white wine

3 tbsp sweet sherry

1 clove garlic, crushed

very easy — serves 4

Skin the salmon and cut the flesh into 5 cm/2 inch chunks. Trim the leeks and cut them into 5 cm/2 inch lengths.

Thread the salmon and leeks alternately onto 8 pre-soaked wooden skewers. Leave to chill in the refrigerator until required.

To make the sauce, place all of the ingredients in a small pan and heat gently, stirring, until the sugar has dissolved.

Bring to the boil, then reduce the heat and simmer for 2 minutes. Strain the sauce through a fine sieve and leave to cool until it is required.

Pour about one-third of the sauce into a small dish and set aside to serve with the kebabs.

Brush plenty of the remaining sauce over the skewers and cook directly on the rack.

If preferred, place a sheet of oiled kitchen foil on the rack and cook the salmon on that.

Barbecue the salmon and leek kebabs over hot coals for about 10 minutes or until cooked through, turning once.

Use a brush to baste frequently during cooking with the remaining sauce in order to prevent the fish and vegetables from drying out. Transfer the kebabs to a large serving platter and serve with a small bowl of the reserved sauce for dipping.

green
fish
curry

1 tbsp vegetable oil

2 spring onions, sliced

1 tsp cumin seeds, ground

2 fresh green chillies, chopped

1 tsp coriander seeds, ground

4 tbsp chopped fresh coriander

4 tbsp chopped fresh mint

1 tbsp snipped fresh chives

150 ml/5 fl oz coconut milk

salt and pepper

4 white fish fillets, about 225 g/8 oz each

fresh mint sprigs, to garnish

freshly cooked basmati rice, to serve

very easy - serves 4

Heat the vegetable oil in a large, heavy-based frying pan, add the spring onions and stir-fry over a medium heat for 2 minutes, or until softened but not coloured. Stir in the ground cumin, chillies and ground coriander and cook until the spices are fragrant.

Add the fresh coriander, mint, chives and coconut milk and season liberally with salt and pepper.

Using a fish slice, carefully place the fish in the frying pan and poach for 10–15 minutes, or until the flesh flakes easily when tested with a fork. Transfer the fish to 4 large, warmed serving plates, garnish with fresh mint sprigs and serve immediately with freshly cooked basmati rice.

350 g/12 oz skinless cod fillet

25 g/1 oz unsalted butter

1 onion, chopped

2 red peppers, deseeded and chopped

4 tomatoes, peeled, deseeded and chopped

8 ready-prepared scallops

2 tbsp olive oil

225 g/8 oz risotto rice

450 ml/16 fl oz hot fish stock

salt

225 g/8 oz cooked peeled prawns

1 tbsp chopped flat-leafed parsley

2 tbsp freshly grated Parmesan cheese

fresh parsley sprigs, to garnish

easy - serves 4

Cut the fish into cubes. Melt half the butter in a large saucepan. Add the onion, red peppers and tomatoes and cook over a low heat, stirring occasionally, for 5 minutes, or until softened. Add the fish and scallops, and cook for a further 3 minutes. Transfer the fish mixture to a plate with a slotted spoon, cover and reserve.

Add the oil to the pan and heat gently. Add the rice and stir to coat with the butter and oil. Stir in a ladleful of stock and season to taste with salt. Cook, stirring, until the stock has been absorbed. Continue cooking and adding stock, a ladleful at a time, for 20 minutes, or until the rice is tender and all of the liquid has been absorbed.

Gently stir in the reserved fish mixture with the prawns and heat through for 2 minutes. Transfer the risotto to a warmed serving dish, sprinkle with the chopped parsley and Parmesan cheese and serve immediately, garnished with parsley sprigs.

seafood risotto

INDEX